foreword

Whether it's for a celebratory gathering or a weekend meal with plenty of weeknight leftovers, a roast makes a stylish statement. From its first heady aroma to your grand entrance with the pièce de résistance, you've given notice that this is a meal that matters.

But for all its panache, a roast is the simplest thing to cook. Add a few ingredients, shoo it into the oven and leave it to do its thing. To make it even easier, we've gathered recipes with less than 10 ingredients (we didn't count salt, pepper and water!) from our Company's Coming library.

Choose from our Savoury Rib Roast or Mushroom Madeira Tenderloin. Or try the Fiery Chipotle Lamb or the Pork Loin with Orange and Sage. Of course, we've also included classic roast chicken and turkey recipes, as well as illustrated directions on pages 60–61 for carving poultry. It's all so effortless with *Easy Roasting*.

Jean Paré

herbed beef tenderloin

Because a roast is so impressive, a sprig or two of fresh herbs is all the garnish you'll need. Other options include grape clusters (choose the same colour as your wine) or even the vegetables you've roasted beside the meat.

Beef tenderloin roast	3 lbs.	1.4 kg
Olive (or cooking) oil	2 tsp.	10 mL
Parsley flakes	2 tsp.	10 mL
Dried thyme	1 1/2 tsp.	7 mL
Salt	1/4 tsp.	1 mL
Coarsely ground pepper	1 tsp.	5 mL
Dried tarragon	1 tsp.	5 mL
Onion powder	1 tsp.	5 mL
Garlic powder	1/2 tsp.	2 mL

Tuck thin end of tenderloin under to make uniform shape, if necessary. Tie with butcher's string. Rub olive oil over tenderloin.

Combine remaining 7 ingredients in small cup. Rub over tenderloin. Place on greased wire rack set in broiler pan. Cook in 425°F (220°C) oven for about 45 minutes until meat thermometer inserted into thickest part of tenderloin reads 160°F (71°C) for medium or until desired doneness. Transfer to cutting board. Cover with foil. Let stand for 10 minutes before carving. Serves 12.

1 serving: 218 Calories; 11.2 g Total Fat (4.8 g Mono, 0.6 g Poly, 3.9 g Sat); 65 mg Cholesterol; 1 g Carbohydrate; trace Fibre; 27 g Protein; 145 mg Sodium

grilled beef tenderloin

Beef tenderloin, called eye fillet in New Zealand and Australia, is, as its name implies, the tenderest cut of beef. Guests will definitely ask for seconds.

Hard margarine (or butter), melted	1/4 cup	60 mL
Red wine vinegar	1 1/2 tsp.	7 mL
Worcestershire sauce	1 tsp.	5 mL
Beef bouillon powder	1/2 tsp.	2 mL
Beef tenderloin roast	2 1/4 lbs.	1 kg

Combine first 4 ingredients in small bowl.

Brush tenderloin with margarine mixture. Preheat gas barbecue to high. Cook tenderloin on greased grill, turning often until browned on all sides. Reduce heat to medium-high. Move tenderloin to 1 side of grill over drip pan. Turn off burner under tenderloin, leaving opposite burner on medium-high. Close lid. Cook for about 60 minutes, turning occasionally and brushing with margarine mixture, until meat thermometer inserted into thickest part of tenderloin reads 160°F (71°C) for medium or until desired doneness. Transfer to cutting board. Cover with foil. Let stand for 10 minutes before carving. Serves 9.

1 serving: 178 Calories; 11.0 g Total Fat (5.6 g Mono, 0.8 g Poly, 3.2 g Sat); 44 mg Cholesterol; 0 g Carbohydrate; 0 g Fibre; 18 g Protein; 144 mg Sodium

beef and pears in wine

Here's an intimate dinner for two...perfect for a romantic evening. To ensure even cooking, remove the beef from the fridge 30 minutes before cooking.

Beef tenderloin roast	1/2 – 3/4 lb.	225 – 340 g
Cooking oil	1 tsp.	5 mL
Pepper, sprinkle		
Cooking oil	2 tsp.	10 mL
Finely chopped onion	2 tbsp.	30 mL
Dry (or alcohol-free) red wine	1 cup	250 mL
Redcurrant jelly	2 tbsp.	30 mL
Dijon mustard	2 tsp.	10 mL
Peeled medium pear, core removed and quartered	1	1

Place tenderloin on greased wire rack set in small roasting pan. Drizzle with first amount of cooking oil. Sprinkle with pepper. Cook, uncovered, in 350°F (175°C) oven for 40 to 45 minutes until meat thermometer inserted in thickest part of tenderloin reads 160°F (71°C) for medium or until desired doneness. Transfer to cutting board. Cover with foil. Let stand for 10 minutes before carving.

Heat second amount of cooking oil in medium saucepan on medium-low. Add onion. Cook for about 5 minutes, stirring often, until onion is softened.

Add next 3 ingredients. Heat and stir on medium for about 4 minutes until jelly is dissolved. Bring to a boil. Reduce heat to medium-low.

Add pear. Simmer, uncovered, for 10 to 15 minutes, stirring occasionally, until pear is tender. Transfer pear to small cup. Cover to keep warm. Strain wine mixture through sieve into same saucepan. Bring to a boil on medium-high. Boil, uncovered, for about 5 minutes, stirring occasionally, until thickened. Serve with tenderloin and pear. Serves 2.

1 serving: 363 Calories; 13.8 g Total Fat (6.7 g Mono, 2.6 g Poly, 3.0 g Sat); 42 mg Cholesterol; 22 g Carbohydrate; 2 g Fibre; 18 g Protein; 133 mg Sodium

mushroom madeira tenderloin

After early trading ships carried Madeira through the tropics and into cooler climes, shippers discovered the fortified wine had improved. Now heating and cooling are part of the process.

Beef tenderloin roast	3 – 3 1/2 lbs.	1.4 – 1.6 kg
Salt, sprinkle		
Pepper, sprinkle		

MUSHROOM MADEIRA SAUCE

Butter	1/4 cup	60 mL
Finely chopped onion	1/2 cup	125 mL
Garlic clove, minced (or 1/4 tsp., 1 mL, powder)	1	1
Sliced fresh brown (or white) mushrooms	4 cups	1 L
All-purpose flour	1/4 cup	60 mL
Prepared beef broth	1 1/4 cups	300 mL
Madeira wine	1/2 cup	125 mL
Salt	1/4 tsp.	1 mL
Pepper	1/4 tsp.	1 mL

Place tenderloin on greased wire rack set in 9 x 13 inch (22 x 33 cm) pan. Sprinkle with salt and pepper. Cook, uncovered, in 475°F (240°C) oven for about 15 minutes until browned. Reduce heat to 325°F (160°C). Cook for about 75 minutes until meat thermometer inserted into thickest part of tenderloin reads 160°F (71°C) for medium or until desired doneness. Transfer to cutting board. Cover with foil. Let stand for 10 minutes before carving.

Mushroom Madeira Sauce: Melt butter in large frying pan on medium. Add onion and garlic. Cook for about 5 minutes, stirring often, until onion is softened.

Add mushrooms. Cook for about 10 minutes, stirring occasionally, until mushrooms are browned and liquid is evaporated.

Add flour. Heat and stir for 1 minute.

Slowly add broth and wine, stirring constantly until smooth. Heat and stir until boiling and thickened. Add salt and pepper. Stir. Makes about 2 2/3 cups (650 mL) sauce. Serve with tenderloin. Serves 10.

1 serving: 239 Calories; 12.4 g Total Fat (4.2 g Mono, 0.5 g Poly, 5.8 g Sat); 63 mg Cholesterol; 6 g Carbohydrate; 1 g Fibre; 22 g Protein; 284 mg Sodium

savoury rib roast

Easy? You'd better believe it! Take five minutes to get this roast in the (preheated) oven, then leave it to roast to tender goodness for 2 1/2 hours. You can substitute a prime rib, if you like.

Beef rib-eye roast	4 lbs.	1.8 kg
Ground thyme	1 tbsp.	15 mL
Dried rosemary, crushed	1 tsp.	5 mL
Ground sage	1 tsp.	5 mL
Salt	1 tsp.	5 mL
Pepper	1 tsp.	5 mL

Place roast, fat-side up, on greased wire rack set in large roasting pan.

Combine remaining 5 ingredients in small cup. Rub over roast. Cook, uncovered, in 325°F (160°C) oven for about 2 1/2 hours until meat thermometer reads 160°F (71°C) for medium or until desired doneness. Transfer to cutting board. Cover with foil. Let stand for 10 minutes before carving. Serves 12.

1 serving: 249 Calories; 16.1 g Total Fat (7.1 g Mono, 0.5 g Poly, 6.9 g Sat); 71 mg Cholesterol; trace Carbohydrate; trace Fibre; 24 g Protein; 258 mg Sodium

sesame pepper-crusted beef roast

Differences in barbecues, outside temperatures and even wind can affect cooking time on the grill. With a large piece of barbecued meat, the only sure-fire way of knowing it's done is by checking the internal temperature with a meat thermometer.

Beef rib-eye roast, trimmed of fat	3 lbs.	1.4 kg
Garlic cloves, halved	3	3
Olive (or cooking) oil	1 tbsp.	15 mL
Sesame seeds	1/4 cup	60 mL
Coarsely crushed whole black peppercorns (see Tip, page 64)	2 tbsp.	30 mL
Curry powder	2 tsp.	10 mL

Cut 6 shallow slits in roast at random. Insert garlic into slits. Rub olive oil on roast.

Combine remaining 3 ingredients in small bowl. Spread on sheet of waxed paper. Press all sides of roast into sesame seed mixture until coated. Preheat gas barbecue to medium-high. Place roast on 1 side of greased grill over drip pan. Turn off burner under roast, leaving opposite burner on medium-high. Close lid. Cook for 30 minutes. Reduce heat to medium. Cook for another 30 minutes until meat thermometer reads 145°F (63°C) for medium-rare or until desired doneness. Transfer to cutting board. Cover with foil. Let stand for 10 minutes before carving. Serves 12.

1 serving: 208 Calories; 10.4 g Total Fat (4.7 g Mono, 1.1 g Poly, 3.4 g Sat); 55 mg Cholesterol; 2 g Carbohydrate; 0 g Fibre; 25 g Protein; 72 mg Sodium

comfort roast with creamy horseradish sauce

Large cuts of meat need to rest for a bit after being removed from the oven. This allows the juices to be evenly distributed and makes the roast easier to carve. Cover the resting roast with foil to keep it warm.

Dijon mustard	3 tbsp.	50 mL
Prepared horseradish	1 tbsp.	15 mL
Garlic clove, minced (or 1/4 tsp., 1 mL, powder)	1	1
Montreal steak spice	1 tsp.	5 mL
Beef sirloin tip roast	3 lbs.	1.4 kg
CREAMY HORSERADISH SAUCE		
Sour cream	1 cup	250 mL
Dijon mustard	1 tbsp.	15 mL
Prepared horseradish	1 tbsp.	15 mL
Lemon juice	1 tsp.	5 mL
Salt	1/4 tsp.	1 mL
Pepper	1/8 tsp.	0.5 mL

Combine first 4 ingredients in small bowl.

Place roast on large plate. Rub mustard mixture over roast. Let stand, covered, in refrigerator for at least 6 hours or overnight. Place roast on greased wire rack set in roasting pan. Cook, uncovered, in 475°F (240°C) oven for about 30 minutes until browned. Reduce heat to 300°F (150°C). Cook for 2 to 2 1/2 hours until meat thermometer reads 160°F (71°C) for medium or until desired doneness. Transfer to cutting board. Cover with foil. Let stand for 10 minutes before carving.

Creamy Horseradish Sauce: Combine all 6 ingredients in small bowl. Makes about 1 cup (250 mL) sauce. Serve with roast. Serves 12.

1 serving plus 2 tbsp. (30 mL) sauce: 208 calories; 11.0 g Total Fat (3.8 g Mono, 0.4 g Poly, 5.3 g Sat); 66 mg Cholesterol; 1 g Carbohydrate; trace Fibre; 24 g Protein; 259 g Sodium

saucy braised beef

Wonderful on crusty rolls or focaccia bread, this dressed up version of beef on a bun can be made the day before, refrigerated, then covered and heated for 20 minutes in a 350°F (175°C) oven, stirring occasionally.

Dried oregano	1 tsp.	5 mL
Salt	1/2 tsp.	2 mL
Pepper	1/4 tsp.	1 mL
Boneless beef brisket roast	2 lbs.	900 g
Garlic cloves, minced	2	2
Large onion, sliced	1	1
Dry (or alcohol-free) red wine (or prepared beef broth)	3/4 cup	175 mL
Ketchup	1/4 cup	60 mL
Sun-dried tomato pesto	2 tbsp.	30 mL

Combine first 3 ingredients in small bowl. Rub over roast. Place, fat-side up, in greased 2 quart (2 L) shallow baking dish.

Spread garlic evenly over top of roast. Top with onion. Cook, uncovered, in 350°F (175°C) oven for about 1 hour until onion starts to brown. Reduce heat to 300°F (150°C).

Pour wine around roast in baking dish. Cook, covered, for 2 to 2 1/2 hours until beef is very tender and pulls apart easily. Scrape onion from roast. Add to drippings. Transfer roast to large bowl. Shred roast with 2 forks. Cover to keep warm.

Skim any fat from surface of drippings. Transfer drippings to blender or food processor. Add ketchup and pesto. Process until smooth (see Safety Tip). Pour over beef. Toss until coated. Serves 8.

1 serving: 177 Calories; 7.7 g Total Fat (3.5 g Mono, 0.3 g Poly, 2.7 g Sat); 44 mg Cholesterol; 5 g Carbohydrate; 1 g Fibre; 18 g Protein; 290 mg Sodium

Safety Tip: Follow manufacturer's instructions for processing hot liquids.

texas pot roast

Browning this less expensive cut of meat under the broiler ensures that all the flavours stay inside. Rice or mashed potatoes would complement the gravy nicely.

Cooking oil	1 tbsp.	15 mL
Boneless beef blade (or chuck) roast	3 1/2 lbs.	1.6 kg
Envelope of taco seasoning mix	1 1/4 oz.	35 g
Can of diced tomatoes (with juice)	14 oz.	398 mL
Can of diced green chilies (with juice)	4 oz.	113 g
Beef bouillon powder	2 tsp.	10 mL
Brown sugar	2 tsp.	10 mL
Water	1/2 cup	125 mL
All-purpose flour	6 tbsp.	100 mL

Rub cooking oil over roast. Sprinkle with taco seasoning. Place in shallow roasting pan. Broil on centre rack in oven for about 10 minutes per side until browned. Transfer to Dutch oven.

Combine next 4 ingredients in small bowl. Pour over roast. Simmer, covered, on medium-low for 2 1/2 hours. Remove roast to cutting board. Cover with foil. Let stand for 10 minutes before carving.

Stir water into flour in small cup until smooth. Bring liquid in Dutch oven to a boil. Slowly add flour mixture, stirring constantly with whisk until boiling and thickened. Serve with roast. Serves 8.

1 serving: 246 Calories; 12.0 g Total Fat (5.4 g Mono, 0.9 g Poly, 4.1 g Sat); 74 mg Cholesterol; 6 g Carbohydrate; 1 g Fibre; 27 g Protein; 564 mg Sodium

teriyaki round roast

A homemade teriyaki sauce enhances this eye of round. Adding water after the heat is reduced prevents scorching. For thicker gravy, shake 2 tsp. (10 mL) cornstarch and 1/4 cup (60 mL) water in a tightly closed jar and add contents to the saucepan.

Dry sherry	1/2 cup	125 mL
Orange juice	1/2 cup	125 mL
Finely chopped onion	1/4 cup	60 mL
Soy sauce	1/4 cup	60 mL
Brown sugar	2 tbsp.	30 mL
Beef bouillon powder	1 tbsp.	15 mL
Finely grated ginger root	2 tsp.	10 mL
Garlic clove, crushed	1	1
Beef eye of round roast	2 lbs.	900 g
Water	1 cup	250 mL

Combine first 8 ingredients in small bowl.

Pierce roast several times with long fork. Put into large resealable freezer bag. Add orange juice mixture. Seal bag. Turn until coated. Let stand in refrigerator for at least 8 hours or overnight, turning occasionally. Reserve orange juice mixture in refrigerator. Place roast on greased rack set in medium roasting pan. Cook, uncovered, in a 500°F (260°C) oven for 30 minutes. Reduce heat to 275°F (140°C).

Add water to roasting pan. Cook, uncovered, for about 1 hour or until meat thermometer reads 160°F (71°C) for medium or until desired doneness. Remove roast to cutting board. Cover with foil. Let stand for 10 minutes before carving. Strain reserved orange juice mixture through sieve into small saucepan. Bring to a boil. Reduce heat to medium. Boil gently for at least 5 minutes. Serve with roast. Serves 8.

1 serving: 184 Calories; 5.5 g Total Fat (3.2 g Mono, 0.2 g Poly, 2.0 g Sat); 45 mg Cholesterol; 7 g Carbohydrate; 1 g Fibre; 23 g Protein; 792 mg Sodium

ruby-glazed roast beef

If your roast weighs more or less than indicated, just calculate 25 minutes per pound (55 minutes per kilogram) for the cooking time after you've reduced the oven temperature. Rarer beef takes less time.

Beef inside round (or eye of round) roast	3 lbs.	1.4 kg
Redcurrant jelly, warmed	1 cup	250 mL
Sun-dried tomatoes, softened in boiling water for 10 minutes before chopping	1/4 cup	60 mL
Italian seasoning	1 tsp.	5 mL
Ground ginger	1/2 tsp.	2 mL
Water	1/4 cup	60 mL
Cornstarch	1 tbsp.	15 mL

Place roast, fat-side up, on greased wire rack set in small roasting pan. Cook, uncovered, in 500°F (260°C) oven for 30 minutes.

Combine next 4 ingredients in small bowl. Pour over roast. Cook, uncovered, in 275° (140°C) oven, brushing several times with pan juices, for about 75 minutes or until meat thermometer reads 160°F (71°C) for medium or until desired doneness. Transfer to cutting board. Cover with foil. Let stand for 10 minutes before carving.

Stir water into cornstarch in small cup. Transfer roasting pan to stove. Bring to a boil. Add cornstarch mixture. Heat and stir on medium until boiling and thickened. Serve with roast. Serves 8.

1 serving: 462 Calories; 10.7 g Total Fat (4.0 g Mono, 0.7 g Poly, 3.6 g Sat); 98 mg Cholesterol; 46 g Carbohydrate; 1 g Fibre; 45 g Protein; 111 mg Sodium

peppercorn roast

Let the roast absorb the peppercorn flavour by applying the rub the day before. The Creamy Horseradish Sauce on page 14 is a delicious accompaniment.

Beef inside round (or rump or sirloin tip) roast	3 1/2 lbs.	1.6 kg
Dijon mustard	2 tbsp.	30 mL
Lemon juice	1 tbsp.	15 mL
Crushed whole black peppercorns (or coarsely ground pepper), see Tip, page 64	2 tsp.	10 mL
Dried oregano	1/2 tsp.	2 mL
Ground cloves	1/2 tsp.	2 mL

Put roast into large bowl.

Combine remaining 5 ingredients in small cup. Rub over roast. Let stand, covered, in refrigerator for at least 8 hours or overnight. Preheat gas barbecue to medium. Place roast on 1 side of greased grill over drip pan. Turn off burner under roast, leaving burner on opposite side on medium. Close lid. Cook for about 2 1/2 hours until meat thermometer reads 160°F (71°C) for medium or until desired doneness. Transfer to cutting board. Cover with foil. Let stand for 10 minutes before carving. Serves 14.

1 serving: 141 Calories; 3.9 g Total Fat (1.6 g Mono, 0.2 g Poly, 1.3 g Sat); 51 mg Cholesterol; trace Carbohydrate; trace Fibre; 25 g Protein; 59 mg Sodium

easy pot roast and gravy

Cooked vegetables form the basis of the gravy for this simple pot roast. Refrigerate any leftovers in a heatproof, covered casserole dish and you're all set for tomorrow's dinner.

Boneless beef blade (or chuck or round) roast	3 lbs.	1.4 kg
Medium carrot, diced	1	1
Chopped onion	1/2 cup	125 mL
Water	2 cups	500 mL
Garlic powder	1/2 tsp.	2 mL
Ground sage	1/2 tsp.	2 mL
Salt	1/2 tsp.	2 mL
Pepper	1/8 tsp.	0.5 mL
All-purpose flour	2 tbsp.	30 mL

Place roast in small roasting pan. Scatter carrot and onion around roast. Pour water over top.

Sprinkle next 4 ingredients over vegetables. Bake, covered, in 350°F (175°C) oven for 2 to 2 1/2 hours until roast is very tender. Transfer to cutting board. Cover with foil. Let stand for 10 minutes before carving.

Process drippings, vegetables and flour in blender or food processor until smooth (see Safety Tip). Transfer to medium saucepan. Heat and stir on medium until boiling and thickened. Makes about 3 1/2 cups (875 mL) gravy. Serve with roast. Serves 8.

1 serving: 402 Calories; 27.5 g Total Fat (11.7 g Mono, 1.1 g Poly, 11.2 g Sat); 94 mg Cholesterol; 4 g Carbohydrate; trace Fibre; 33 g Protein; 265 mg Sodium

Safety Tip: Follow manufacturer's instructions for processing hot liquids.

slow-roasted lamb

Tuck this into your oven on a chilly afternoon and call up a few friends for a warm, relaxing evening of entertaining. Couscous and steamed vegetables would round out the menu nicely.

Leg of lamb, trimmed of fat	4 lbs.	1.8 kg
Garlic cloves, quartered	3	3
Olive (or cooking) oil	1 tbsp.	15 mL
Dry (or alcohol-free) red wine	1/2 cup	125 mL
Low-sodium prepared chicken broth	1/2 cup	125 mL
Balsamic vinegar	1/4 cup	60 mL
Brown sugar, packed	2 tbsp.	30 mL
Salt	1/2 tsp.	2 mL

Cut 12 shallow slits in roast at random. Insert garlic pieces into slits.

Heat olive oil in large frying pan on medium-high. Add roast. Cook for about 8 minutes, turning often, until browned. Transfer to small roasting pan.

Add remaining 5 ingredients to same frying pan. Heat and stir on medium, scraping any brown bits from bottom of pan, until brown sugar is dissolved. Pour wine mixture over lamb. Bake, covered, in 250°F (120°C) oven for 4 to 4 1/2 hours, turning every hour, until roast is tender. Transfer to cutting board. Cover with foil. Let stand for 15 minutes before carving. Skim and discard fat from liquid in roasting pan. Transfer liquid to small saucepan. Bring to a boil. Boil, uncovered, for 5 to 10 minutes until reduced by half. Makes about 1 1/4 cups (300 mL) sauce. Serve with roast. Serves 6.

1 serving: *306 Calories; 11.0 g Total Fat (5.2 g Mono, 1.0 g Poly, 3.4 g Sat);*
124 mg Cholesterol; 6 g Carbohydrate; trace Fibre; 40 g Protein; 374 mg Sodium

fiery chipotle lamb

Chipotle (chih-POHT-lay) peppers are smoked jalapeño chili peppers. Canned in adobo sauce, they're often found in the Mexican section of your grocery store. You can freeze the remainder in recipe-friendly quantities. Wash your hands well after handling them.

CHIPOTLE RUB

Cooking oil	1 tbsp.	15 mL
Chopped onion	1 cup	250 mL
Garlic cloves, minced (or 1/2 tsp., 2 mL, powder)	2	2
Mayonnaise	1/3 cup	75 mL
Chipotle peppers in adobo sauce	2	2
Granulated sugar	1 tbsp.	15 mL
Salt	1/2 tsp.	2 mL
Leg of lamb	3 1/3 lbs.	1.5 kg

Chipotle Rub: Heat cooking oil in medium frying pan on medium-low. Add onion and garlic. Cook for about 10 minutes, stirring often, until onion is softened. Transfer to blender or food processor.

Add next 4 ingredients. Process until smooth. Makes about 3/4 cup (175 mL) rub.

Put roast into large shallow dish. Spread Chipotle Rub over roast. Let stand, covered, in refrigerator for at least 8 hours or overnight. Preheat gas barbecue to high. Place roast on 1 side of greased grill over drip pan. Turn off burner under roast, leaving opposite burner on high. Close lid. Cook for about 2 hours or until meat thermometer inserted into thickest part of leg reads 160°F (71°C) for medium or until desired doneness. Transfer to cutting board. Cover with foil. Let stand for 10 minutes before carving. Serves 6.

1 serving: 642 Calories; 45.1 g Total Fat (20.8 g Mono, 6.5 g Poly, 14.7 g Sat); 190 mg Cholesterol; 5 g Carbohydrate; 1 g Fibre; 51 g Protein; 395 mg Sodium

garlic rosemary lamb

If you want a little more spice in your life, add extra crushed chilies. A saffron-coloured pilaf, or even a mix of wild and regular rice, would make this a feast for the eyes and the palate.

Chopped fresh parsley	1/4 cup	60 mL
Olive (or cooking) oil	2 tbsp.	30 mL
Garlic cloves, minced	6	6
Finely chopped fresh rosemary	1 tbsp.	15 mL
(or 3/4 tsp., 4 mL, dried, crushed)		
Liquid honey	1 tbsp.	15 mL
Grated lemon zest	2 tsp.	10 mL
Salt	1/2 tsp.	2 mL
Dried crushed chilies	1/4 tsp.	1 mL
Rack of lamb (4 to 6 ribs)	3/4 lbs.	340 g

Combine first 8 ingredients in small bowl.

Cover tips of bones of lamb rack with foil, if desired, to prevent darkening. Press parsley mixture onto each side of lamb rack. Let stand for 20 minutes. Preheat small roasting pan in 475°F (240°C) oven for 5 minutes. Place lamb rack, bone-side down, on greased wire rack set in same roasting pan. Cook, uncovered, for 10 minutes. Reduce heat to 375°F (190°C). Cook, covered, for about 20 minutes until meat thermometer inserted into thickest part of lamb rack reads 155°F (68°C) or until desired doneness. Transfer to cutting board. Cover with foil. Let stand for 10 minutes before cutting. Internal temperature should rise to at least 160°F (71°C). Cut between ribs to serve. Serves 2.

1 serving: 517 Calories; 42.4 g Total Fat (22.1 g Mono, 3.3 g Poly, 14.1 g Sat); 93 mg Cholesterol; 13 g Carbohydrate; trace Fibre; 21 g Protein; 673 mg Sodium

cranberry apple pork roast

Cranberries aren't just for Christmas, though the holiday season is the right time to pick up inexpensive packages of fresh berries. Toss them in your freezer for delicious recipes such as this one.

Boneless pork loin roast	4 – 4 1/2 lbs.	1.8 – 2 kg
Salt	1/4 tsp.	1 mL
Pepper	1/4 tsp.	1 mL
CRANBERRY APPLE SAUCE		
Frozen (or fresh) cranberries, thawed	3 cups	750 mL
Chopped peeled cooking apple (such as McIntosh)	2 cups	500 mL
Liquid honey	1/2 cup	125 mL
Frozen concentrated apple juice, thawed	3 tbsp.	50 mL
Chopped fresh jalapeño pepper (see Tip, page 64)	2 tbsp.	30 mL
Finely chopped ginger root	1 tbsp.	15 mL
Grated lime zest	1 tsp.	5 mL

Put pork into large roasting pan. Sprinkle with salt and pepper. Cook, uncovered, in 400°F (205°C) oven for 30 minutes. Reduce heat to 325°F (160°C). Cook, uncovered, for about 45 minutes until meat thermometer inserted into thickest part reads 160°F (71°C) for medium or until desired doneness. Transfer to cutting board. Cover with foil. Let stand for 10 minutes before carving.

Cranberry Apple Sauce: Combine all 7 ingredients in medium saucepan. Bring to a boil. Reduce heat to medium. Boil gently, uncovered, for about 10 minutes, stirring occasionally, until cranberries are soft. Makes about 3 cups (750 mL) sauce. Serve with pork. Serves 12.

1 serving: 340 Calories; 15.4 g Total Fat (6.7 g Mono, 1.4 g Poly, 5.8 g Sat); 91 mg Cholesterol; 19 g Carbohydrate; 2 g Fibre; 30 g Protein; 122 mg Sodium

pork loin with orange and sage

Before you cut the string of the pork, count the number of times it goes around the meat. That will guide you in retying the roast once it's been stuffed. Garnish with orange slices and fresh sage.

Hard margarine (or butter), softened	3 tbsp.	50 mL
Dijon mustard	2 tbsp.	30 mL
Finely grated orange zest	2 tsp.	10 mL
Boneless pork loin roast	4 1/2 lbs.	2 kg
Bacon slices	6	6
Fresh sage leaves, firmly packed	1/3 cup	75 mL
Cooking oil	2 tsp.	10 mL
Salt	1 tsp.	5 mL

Combine first 3 ingredients in small bowl.

Cut strings from pork. Unroll pork, fat-side down, on cutting board. Spread with mustard mixture.

Layer bacon slices and sage over mustard mixture. Roll up pork, jelly-roll style, to enclose filling. Tie with butcher's string. Drizzle with cooking oil. Sprinkle with salt. Preheat gas barbecue to medium-high. Place pork on 1 side of greased grill over drip pan. Turn off burner under pork, leaving opposite burner on medium-high. Close lid. Cook for 30 minutes. Turn pork. Reduce heat to medium. Close lid. Cook for 1 hour until meat thermometer inserted into thickest part reads 160°F (71°C) for medium or until desired doneness. Transfer to cutting board. Cover with foil. Let stand for 10 minutes before carving. Serves 12.

1 serving: 298 Calories; 16.4 g Total Fat (6.9 g Mono, 1.4 g Poly, 6.5 g Sat); 107 mg Cholesterol; trace Carbohydrate; trace Fibre; 35 g Protein; 388 mg Sodium

garlic-stuffed pork roast

Garlic lovers will adore the "treasures" they discover embedded in their slices of meat. Pop a pan of baby potatoes drizzled with olive oil into the oven for the last 50 minutes or so as a convenient accompaniment.

Boneless pork loin roast	3 1/2 lbs.	1.6 kg
Garlic cloves, cut in half	8	8
Pepper	3/4 tsp.	4 mL
Dried oregano	1/4 tsp.	1 mL
Dried rosemary	1/4 tsp.	1 mL
Dried thyme	1/4 tsp.	1 mL
Parsley flakes	1/4 tsp.	1 mL
HERB GRAVY		
Water	1 cup	250 mL
All-purpose flour	2 tbsp.	30 mL
Pan drippings without fat, plus water to make	1 cup	250 mL

Cut 16 shallow slits in pork at random. Insert garlic pieces into slits. Put into small roasting pan.

Combine remaining 5 ingredients in small bowl. Rub over pork. Cook, covered, in 400°F (205°C) oven for 20 minutes. Reduce heat to 325°F (160°C). Cook, covered, for 1 1/2 to 2 hours until meat thermometer inserted into centre of pork reads 160°F (71°C) for medium or until desired doneness. Transfer to cutting board. Cover with foil. Let stand for 10 minutes before carving.

Herb Gravy: Stir first amount of water into flour in small bowl until smooth. Put drippings, and water if necessary, into small saucepan. Bring to a boil. Add flour mixture, stirring constantly with whisk. Heat and stir on medium for 5 to 7 minutes until boiling and thickened. Makes about 2 cups (500 mL) gravy. Serve with pork. Serves 6.

1 serving: 121 Calories; 4.5 g Total Fat (2.0 g Mono, 0.5 g Poly, 1.6 g Sat); 47 mg Cholesterol; 2 g Carbohydrate; trace Fibre; 17 g Protein; 42 mg Sodium

easy chinese bbq pork

Here's that tasty red-glazed pork from your favourite Asian restaurant.
Serve this with a side of chow mein.

Hoisin sauce	3 tbsp.	50 mL
Dry sherry	2 tbsp.	30 mL
Liquid honey	2 tbsp.	30 mL
Soy sauce	2 tbsp.	30 mL
Oyster sauce	1 tbsp.	15 mL
Chinese five-spice powder	1/4 tsp.	1 mL
Red liquid food colouring (optional)	1/4 tsp.	1 mL
Pork tenderloins (3/4 – 1 lb., 340 – 454 g, each), trimmed of fat and halved lengthwise	2	2
Liquid honey	1 tbsp.	15 mL
Water	1 tbsp.	15 mL
Sesame oil (for flavour)	2 tsp.	10 mL
Drops of red liquid food colouring (optional)	2	2

Combine first 7 ingredients in small bowl.

Put tenderloins into large resealable freezer bag. Add hoisin mixture. Seal bag. Turn until coated. Let stand in refrigerator for 4 hours, turning occasionally. Remove tenderloins. Transfer hoisin mixture to small saucepan. Bring to a boil. Boil, covered, for at least 5 minutes. Pour water into broiler pan until 1/2 inch (12 mm) deep. Place tenderloins on greased wire rack set in broiler pan. Brush tenderloins with boiled hoisin mixture. Broil on centre rack in oven for about 10 minutes, turning and brushing with boiled hoisin mixture at halftime, until browned. Cook in 400°F (205°C) oven for 5 minutes, brushing with boiled hoisin mixture once.

Combine remaining 4 ingredients in small bowl. Transfer half to small cup. Brush remaining honey mixture over tenderloins. Broil for about 5 minutes, turning and brushing at halftime with reserved honey mixture, until dull reddish-brown colour and meat thermometer inserted into thickest part of tenderloins reads 160°F (71°C) or until desired doneness. Transfer to cutting board. Cover with foil. Let stand for 10 minutes before carving. Serves 8.

1 serving: 162 Calories; 4.9 g Total Fat (2.1 g Mono, 1.0 g Poly, 1.4 g Sat); 54 mg Cholesterol; 9 g Carbohydrate; trace Fibre; 18 g Protein; 350 mg Sodium

whisky molasses-glazed ham

For impressive entrees, you can't beat a whole roasted ham, especially with a sweet, smoky glaze. Leftovers make fabulous sandwiches, while the bone can be the start of a tasty homemade soup.

WHISKY MOLASSES GLAZE

Frozen concentrated orange juice, thawed	1/2 cup	125 mL
Peach jam	1/3 cup	75 mL
Fancy (mild) molasses	1/4 cup	60 mL
Canadian whisky (rye)	3 tbsp.	50 mL
Dijon mustard	2 tbsp.	30 mL
Coarsely ground pepper	1 1/2 tsp.	7 mL
Partially cooked skinless ham (bone-in), fat trimmed to 1/4 inch (6 mm) thick	8 – 10 lbs.	3.6 – 4.5 kg

Whisky Molasses Glaze: Combine first 6 ingredients in small saucepan. Bring to a boil on medium. Reduce heat to medium-low. Simmer, uncovered, for about 15 minutes until thickened. Makes about 1 cup (250 mL) glaze.

Put ham into large roasting pan. Cook, covered, in 325°F (160°C) oven for about 2 hours until meat thermometer inserted in thickest part of ham reads 130°F (54°C). Brush ham with half of glaze. Cook, uncovered, for about 1 hour, brushing with remaining glaze every 15 minutes, until meat thermometer inserted into thickest part of ham reads 160°F (71°C). Transfer to cutting board. Cover with foil. Let stand for 10 minutes. Brush with pan juices. Serves 12.

1 serving: 393 Calories; 14.6 g Total Fat (6.9 g Mono, 1.3 g Poly, 5.1 g Sat); 145 mg Cholesterol; 15 g Carbohydrate; trace Fibre; 46 g Protein; 134 mg Sodium

redcurrant-and-mustard-glazed ham

Five ingredients are all you need to feed a large gathering with this magnificent ham. Add mashed potatoes and a salad or two and you'll garner praise for being able to entertain so effortlessly.

REDCURRANT MUSTARD GLAZE

Redcurrant jelly	1/2 cup	125 mL
Apple cider vinegar	1/4 cup	60 mL
Dry mustard	1 tbsp.	15 mL
Cooked ham (bone-in)	9 lbs.	4 kg
Whole cloves, approximately	3 tbsp.	50 mL

Redcurrant Mustard Glaze: Combine first 3 ingredients in small saucepan. Heat and stir on medium for about 5 minutes until jelly is dissolved. Set aside. Makes about 3/4 cup (175 mL) glaze.

Score ham in diamond shape pattern, about 1/4 inch (6 mm) deep with sharp knife. Push cloves into centre of diamonds. Place ham on wire rack set in large roasting pan. Cook in 325°F (160°C) oven for 1 hour. Brush ham with half of glaze. Bake for another 30 to 45 minutes, brushing with remaining glaze several times, until internal temperature reaches 160°F (71°C) and ham is glazed and golden brown. Transfer to cutting board. Cover with foil. Let stand for 10 minutes before carving. Serves 16.

1 serving: 382 Calories; 24.5 g Total Fat (11.5 g Mono, 2.6 g Poly, 8.7 g Sat); 90 mg Cholesterol; 7 g Carbohydrate; 0 g Fibre; 31 g Protein; 1749 mg Sodium

roasted spice chicken

The nice thing about a whole chicken is that you can offer a choice of dark or white meat (see our carving tips, page 60). Save the bones for chicken stock—just freeze them until there's time to simmer up something tasty.

GARLIC ORANGE PASTE

Garlic cloves, minced	4	4
Balsamic vinegar	1 tbsp.	15 mL
Butter (or hard margarine), softened	1 tbsp.	15 mL
Dried oregano	1 tbsp.	15 mL
Frozen concentrated orange juice, thawed	1 tbsp.	15 mL
Ground cumin	1 tbsp.	15 mL
Salt	1 tsp.	5 mL
Pepper	1 tsp.	5 mL
Whole chicken	3 lbs.	1.4 kg
Butter (or hard margarine), softened	1 tsp.	5 mL

Garlic Orange Paste: Stir first 8 ingredients in small bowl until mixture forms a smooth paste. Makes about 1/3 cup (75 mL) paste.

Carefully loosen chicken skin on breasts and thighs but do not remove. Stuff paste between meat and skin, spreading mixture as evenly as possible. Tie wings with butcher's string close to body. Tie legs to tail. Transfer to greased wire rack set in small roasting pan.

Rub second amount of butter over chicken. Cook, covered, in 350°F (175°C) oven for 1 1/4 to 1 1/2 hours until meat thermometer inserted into thickest part of thigh reads 180°F (83°C). Remove chicken from oven. Transfer to cutting board. Remove and discard butcher's string. Cover with foil. Let stand for 10 minutes before carving. Serves 4.

1 serving: 446 Calories; 26.2 g Total Fat (9.6 g Mono, 5.0 g Poly, 8.5 g Sat); 152 mg Cholesterol; 5 g Carbohydrate; 1 g Fibre; 45 g Protein; 750 mg Sodium

butterflied chicken

Butterflying the bird ensures that the meat cooks evenly and quickly on the barbecue. Delicious with potato salad and colourful slices of pepper.

Chopped fresh basil (or 1 1/2 tsp., 7 mL, dried)	2 tbsp.	30 mL
Chopped fresh parsley (or 1 1/2 tsp., 7 mL, flakes)	2 tbsp.	30 mL
Hard margarine (or butter), softened	2 tbsp.	30 mL
Dijon mustard (with whole seeds)	1 tbsp.	15 mL
Salt	1/2 tsp.	2 mL
Coarsely ground pepper	1/2 tsp.	2 mL
Whole chicken	4 lbs.	1.8 kg

Combine first 6 ingredients in small bowl.

Place chicken, backbone-up, on cutting board. Cut down both sides of backbone with kitchen shears or sharp knife to remove (photo 1). Turn chicken over. Press out flat (photo 2). Carefully loosen skin on breast and thighs but do not remove. Stuff herb mixture between meat and skin, spreading mixture as evenly as possible. Preheat gas barbecue to medium. Place chicken, skin-side down, on 1 side of greased grill over drip pan. Turn off burner under chicken, leaving opposite burner on medium. Close lid. Cook for 45 minutes. Turn chicken. Cook for another 40 to 45 minutes until meat thermometer inserted into thickest part of thigh reads 180°F (83°C). Transfer to cutting board. Cover with foil. Let stand for 10 minutes before carving. Serves 4.

1 serving: 483 Calories; 30.3 g Total Fat (13.3 g Mono, 6.0 g Poly, 8.0 g Sat); 157 mg Cholesterol; 1 g Carbohydrate; trace Fibre; 49 g Protein; 564 mg Sodium

classic roast chicken

You can play with the stuffing ingredients by adding two coarsely grated apples for an Apple Stuffing, or 1 lb. (454 g) scramble-fried sausage meat for Sausage Stuffing. Once you see how easy this is, you'll volunteer to make the holiday turkey (on page 58)!

NO-FUSS STUFFING

Coarse dry bread crumbs	6 cups	1.5 L
Onion flakes	1/4 cup	60 mL
Parsley flakes	1 tbsp.	15 mL
Poultry seasoning	2 tsp.	10 mL
Celery salt	1/2 tsp.	2 mL
Salt	1 tsp.	5 mL
Pepper	1/4 tsp.	1 mL
Water	1 1/2 cups	375 mL
Hard margarine (or butter), melted	1/4 cup	60 mL
Whole chicken	6 lbs.	2.7 kg

POULTRY GRAVY

Fat (or cooking oil) from pan drippings	1/2 cup	125 mL
All-purpose flour	1/2 cup	125 mL
Pan drippings, plus water to make	4 cups	1 L
Salt	1 tsp.	5 mL
Pepper	1/4 tsp.	1 mL

No-Fuss Stuffing: Combine first 7 ingredients in large bowl.

Add water and melted margarine. Stir. Add more water, if needed, until stuffing is moist and holds together when squeezed.

Loosely fill body cavity of chicken with stuffing. Secure with wooden picks or small metal skewers. Tie wings with butcher's string close to body. Tie legs to tail. Transfer to medium roasting pan. Cook, covered, in 400°F (205°C) oven for 20 minutes. Reduce heat to 325°F (160°C). Cook for another 2 to 2 1/2 hours until tender and meat thermometer inserted into thickest part of thigh (not stuffing) reads 180°F (83°C). Remove cover for last few minutes of cooking to brown, if needed. Transfer to cutting board. Transfer stuffing to serving dish. Cover to keep warm. Cover chicken with foil. Let stand for 10 minutes before carving.

Poultry Gravy: Heat fat from drippings in medium saucepan on medium until hot. Add flour. Heat and stir for about 1 minute until bubbling. Slowly add drippings and water, stirring constantly. Heat and stir for about 10 minutes until boiling and thickened. Add salt and pepper. Stir. Makes about 4 cups (1 L) gravy. Serve with chicken and stuffing. Serves 8.

1 serving: 928 Calories; 45.8 g Total Fat (18.0 g Mono, 9.1 g Poly, 14.9 g Sat); 190 mg Cholesterol; 70 g Carbohydrate; 4 g Fibre; 55 g Protein; 1631 mg Sodium

cajun roast chicken

Roasted poultry doesn't always need to be stuffed. Here, we've placed an onion in the cavity for flavour, and added some aromatic spices to the skin for oomph. If you'd like gravy, follow the instructions for Poultry Gravy on page 50.

Cooking oil	2 tbsp.	30 mL
Paprika	1 tbsp.	15 mL
Dried oregano	1 1/2 tsp.	7 mL
Dried thyme	1 1/2 tsp.	7 mL
Salt	1 tsp.	5 mL
Garlic powder	1/2 tsp.	2 mL
Cayenne pepper	1/4 tsp.	1 mL
Medium onion, cut in half	1	1
Whole chicken	4 lbs.	1.8 kg

Combine first 7 ingredients in small cup.

Put onion into body cavity of chicken. Rub spice mixture over chicken. Tie wings with butcher's string close to body. Tie legs to tail. Place chicken, breast-side up, on greased wire rack set in small roasting pan. Cook, covered, in 375°F (190°C) oven for about 1 1/2 hours until meat thermometer inserted into thickest part of thigh reads 180°F (83°C). Transfer to cutting board. Cover with foil. Let stand for 10 minutes before carving. Serves 6.

1 serving: 331 Calories; 21.0 g Total Fat (9.1 g Mono, 5.0 g Poly, 4.9 g Sat); 105 mg Cholesterol; 1 g Carbohydrate; trace Fibre; 33 g Protein; 494 mg Sodium

roasted cornish hens

A breed of small chicken, Cornish hen add a touch of elegance to a dinner plate. The cinnamon and sage hint at the exotic.

Cornish hens (about 1 1/2 lbs., 680 g, each)	2	2
BEER MARINADE		
Beer (or alcohol-free beer)	1 cup	250 mL
Applesauce	1/2 cup	125 mL
Liquid honey	2 tbsp.	30 mL
Olive (or cooking) oil	2 tbsp.	30 mL
Paprika	1 tsp.	5 mL
Ground sage	3/4 tsp.	4 mL
Ground cinnamon	1/2 tsp.	2 mL
Salt	1/4 tsp.	1 mL

Place 1 hen, backbone-side up, on cutting board. Cut down both sides of backbone with kitchen shears or sharp knife to remove. Turn hen over. Cut lengthwise through breast into halves. Repeat with remaining hen.

Beer Marinade: Combine all 8 ingredients in large bowl. Makes about 1 3/4 cups (425 mL) marinade. Add hen halves. Turn until coated. Let stand, covered, in refrigerator for at least 6 hours or overnight, turning occasionally. Drain beer mixture into small saucepan. Bring to a boil on medium. Reduce heat to medium-low. Simmer, uncovered, for at least 5 minutes. Preheat gas barbecue to high. Place hen halves, bone-side down, on 1 side of greased grill. Turn off burner under hen halves, leaving opposite burner on medium. Brush hen halves with boiled beer mixture. Close lid. Cook for 20 minutes. Turn. Close lid. Cook for about 20 minutes, turning occasionally and brushing with boiled beer mixture, until browned and no longer pink inside. Transfer to cutting board. Cover with foil. Let stand for 10 minutes. Serves 4.

1 serving: 435 Calories; 27.8 g Total Fat (14.2 g Mono, 4.8 g Poly, 6.7 g Sat); 150 mg Cholesterol; 15 g Carbohydrate; 1 g Fibre; 26 g Protein; 226 mg Sodium

breast of turkey roast

Low-fat, boneless, skinless turkey breasts make the carving easy. Butcher's string can help hold the pieces together.

HERB STUFFING

Fine dry bread crumbs	2 cups	500 mL
Garlic powder	1/8 tsp.	0.5 mL
Ground rosemary	1/8 tsp.	0.5 mL
Ground thyme	1/8 tsp.	0.5 mL
Large egg, fork-beaten	1	1
Hard margarine (or butter), melted	1 tbsp.	15 mL
Water	1 tbsp.	15 mL
Boneless, skinless turkey breasts (1 1/2 lbs., 680 g, each)	2	2

GRAVY

Pan drippings, plus water to make	2 1/2 cups	625 mL
Water	2/3 cup	150 mL
All-purpose flour	6 tbsp.	100 mL
Liquid gravy browner	1/4 tsp.	1 mL
Salt	1/8 tsp.	0.5 mL
Pepper	1/8 tsp.	0.5 mL

Herb Stuffing: Combine first 4 ingredients in medium bowl. Add next 3 ingredients. Mix well.

Place turkey between 2 sheets of plastic wrap. Pound with mallet or rolling pin to flatten slightly. Spoon stuffing onto 1 breast. Spread evenly. Cover with second breast. Press edges together. Place in greased roasting pan. Bake, covered, in 325°F (160°C) oven for about 1 1/2 hours until meat thermometer inserted in thickest part of turkey (not stuffing) reads 180°F (83°C). Transfer to cutting board. Cover with foil. Let stand for 10 minutes before carving.

Gravy: Return drippings and first amount of water to same roasting pan. Transfer to stove. Bring to a boil on medium.

Stir second amount of water into flour in small cup until smooth. Add to drippings, whisking constantly until boiling and thickened.

Add remaining 3 ingredients. Stir. Makes about 3 cups (750 mL) gravy. Serve with roast. Serves 8.

1 serving: 346 Calories; 4.6 g Total Fat (1.9 g Mono, 1.0 g Poly, 1.2 g Sat); 133 mg Cholesterol; 26 g Carbohydrate; 1 g Fibre; 47 g Protein; 370 mg Sodium

roast turkey

Nothing's easier than roasting a turkey, especially without the stuffing. If you'd rather stuff your turkey, omit the onion and check our Roasting Times chart, page 60. You can simmer the neck and giblets in the water that will eventually make the gravy (follow the Poultry Gravy recipe, page 50).

Medium onion, quartered	1	1
Whole turkey, giblets and neck removed (not self-basting)	12 – 15 lbs.	5.4 – 6.8 kg
Cooking oil	2 tbsp.	30 mL

Put onion into body cavity of turkey. Tie wings with butcher's string close to body. Tie legs to tail. Place on greased wire rack set in large roasting pan.

Rub cooking oil over turkey. Cook, covered, in 325°F (160°C) oven for 3 1/4 hours. Cook, uncovered, for about 15 minutes until browned and meat thermometer inserted into thickest part of thigh reads 165°F (74°C). Transfer to cutting board. Cover with foil. Let stand for 15 minutes before carving. Serves 12.

1 serving: 597 Calories; 31.0 g Total Fat (11.7 g Mono, 7.8 g Poly, 8.3 g Sat); 244 mg Cholesterol; 1 g Carbohydrate; trace Fibre; 73 g Protein; 233 mg Sodium

turkey tips

Trussing the turkey: Presenting a gorgeous roast turkey at the table is easier than you think. It starts with properly trussing, or tying, the turkey legs and wings to prevent them from drying out. Stuff the bird, if desired. Loop a piece of butcher's string around each leg, tie them together, and then tie the legs to the tail (photo 1). A separate string around the body of the bird will tuck the wings against the breast.

Roasting times: These are general guidelines for turkeys of various weights, based on a preheated oven. Please note, however, that a turkey is only truly cooked when it reaches its safe internal temperature as indicated in the recipe. Based on a preheated 325°F (160°C) standard oven, these are estimated cooking times:

Size	Without Stuffing	With Stuffing
6 – 8 lbs (3 – 3.5 kg)	2 1/2 – 2 3/4 hours	3 – 3 1/4 hours
8 – 10 lbs (3.5 – 4.5 kg)	2 3/4 – 3 hours	3 1/4 – 3 1/2 hours
10 – 12 lbs (4.5 – 5.5 kg)	3 – 3 1/4 hours	3 1/2 – 3 3/4 hours
12 – 16 lbs (5.5 – 7 kg)	3 1/4 – 3 1/2 hours	3 3/4 – 4 hours
16 – 22 lbs (7 – 10 kg)	3 1/2 – 4 hours	4 – 4 1/2 hours

Carving at the table: Once the turkey's out of the oven, cut the strings, remove the stuffing to a separate bowl and let the turkey rest. Arrange on a platter. At the table, insert a fork into a thigh. Place a sharp knife between the thigh and body of the turkey and cut through the skin of the joint. Use the point of the knife to work through the joint and place it on a cutting board. Cut meat from the thigh and leg, making slices roughly parallel to the bone (photo 2).

Make a horizontal cut just above the wing, slicing through just to the bone of the rib cage. This is your base cut (photo 3).

Starting at one end of the breast, cut off thin slices of meat (photo 4). Alternately, place blade lengthwise about halfway up the breast and slice straight down with an even stroke. Continue to slice breast meat, starting the cut higher for each slice. Repeat procedure on opposite side.

Carving in the kitchen: Remove and slice leg as above. For breast meat, slice down along breastbone following the rib cage to remove the entire breast (photo 5). Slice the breast across the grain into thin slices (photo 6) and place, with the dark meat, on a heated platter.

Carving at the table

Carving in the kitchen

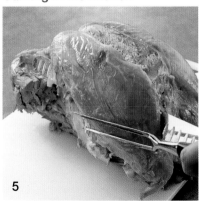

recipe index

topical tips

Bacterial prevention: It is important to clean the cutting board and any utensils used to cut raw chicken, fish or meat in hot, soapy water immediately after use. This will prevent bacteria from spreading to other food.

Chopping jalapeño peppers: Hot peppers contain capsaicin in the seeds and ribs. Removing the seeds and ribs will reduce the heat. Wear protective gloves when handling jalapeño peppers. Do not touch your face near eyes.

Crushing peppercorns: Place whole peppercorns in a small plastic bag. Tap peppercorns with a heavy object, such as a meat mallet or hammer, until coarsely crushed.

Doneness for roast beef and lamb

Medium-rare	145°F (63°C)
Medium	160°F (71°C)
Well done	170°F (77°C)

Nutrition Information Guidelines

Each recipe is analyzed using the Canadian Nutrient File from Health Canada, which is based on the United States Department of Agriculture (USDA) Nutrient Database.

- If more than one ingredient is listed (such as "butter or hard margarine"), or if a range is given (1 – 2 tsp., 5 – 10 mL), only the first ingredient or first amount is analyzed.

- For meat, poultry and fish, the serving size per person is based on the recommended 4 oz. (113 g) uncooked weight (without bone), which is 2 – 3 oz. (57 – 85 g) cooked weight (without bone)— approximately the size of a deck of playing cards.

- Milk used is 1% M.F. (milk fat), unless otherwise stated.

- Cooking oil used is canola oil, unless otherwise stated.

- Ingredients indicating "sprinkle," "optional" or "for garnish" are not included in the nutrition information.

- The fat in recipes and combination foods can vary greatly depending on the sources and types of fats used in each specific ingredient. For these reasons, the count of saturated, monounsaturated and polyunsaturated fats may not add up to the total fat content.